The

Princess

Written By

Monique Hatem Hamatie

April 18th 2012

The

Zahle

Princess

Written By

Monique Hatem Hamatie

Published By LuLu Press International

Nashville - Tennessee

The short stories, prayers and recipes are the collective words of

Monique Hatem Hamatie

This is a non-fiction story about her life.

I would like to dedicate

This project to Jesus Christ!

First and foremost, without the ***LOVE*** of **Jesus**, who I have always believed in, I would not have been able to prepare such inspirational words, such short stories, and such wonderful memories, all for your enjoyment. – Monique,

'The **Zahle** Princess'

The **Zahle** Princess is a collection of short stories about the life of Monique Hatem Hamatie. Included are some of Monique's favorite poems that she wrote herself and others that she has always cherished, along with a collection of some of Monique's favorite Lebanese recipes.

This book has been written by Monique Hatem Hamatie

Introduction...

'Monique' What a name! When some people hear the name, they think of it as a French name, while others enjoy the exotic and international flavor of the name. Whether it is in Lebanon, or in Florida, many people have often said, 'The world only knows of 'one' Monique. She is a lady with many characteristics. The greatest one of these characteristics is 'being humble'. At her recent 60th birthday party, one of Monique's oldest and dearest friends, Rita Gazil, was quoted as saying 'in my years, I haven't met anyone as special as Monique'. Monique Hatem Hamatie in her own way is one of the kindest and sweetest, most compassionate people one could ever have as a friend.

It is my pleasure to have helped in creating this project for her. The following stories you will read today are the personal words, stories and more that truly will tell you about this special lady.

Cathleen Botega – April, 18th 2012

-Editor-

Before I begin sharing the story of the first 60 years of my life, I would like to begin with one of my favorite and most cherished prayers...

All my love and enjoy!

Monique...

----- Saint Jude -----

St. Jude was one of the twelve Apostles. Saint Mark's (3:18) and Saint Matthew's (10:3) gospels refer to him as Thaddeus (a surname meaning "amiable or "loving"), possibly in part to distinguish him from Judas Iscariot, our Lord's betrayer! Saint John's gospel refers to him in the last supper as "Judas... not the Iscariot" (14:22).

The evangelist no doubt wanted to make sure that he would not be confused with the man Jesus Himself referred to as the "son of perdition" in Saint John 17:11!

Oh glorious apostle St. Jude, faithful servant and friend of Jesus, the name of the traitor who delivered thy beloved Master into the hands of His enemies has caused thee to be forgotten by many, but the Church honors and invokes thee universally as the patron of hopeless cases--of things despaired of. Pray for me who am so miserable; make use, I implore thee, of that particular privilege accorded thee of bringing visible and speedy help where help is almost despaired of. Come to my assistance in this great need, that I may receive the consolations and succor of heaven in all my necessities, tribulations and sufferings, particularly (mention your request), and that I may bless God with thee and all the elect throughout eternity. I promise thee, O blessed St. Jude, to be ever mindful of this great favor, and I will never cease to honor thee as my special and powerful patron, and to do all in my power to encourage devotion to thee.

Amen

-Zahle-

- Growing up in the 'Arouse el Bekkah' 'the Bekkah Valley' -

It was my humble honor to enter this world on a very special day in the beginning of winter, 1951. Around Lebanon, and around the entire world, millions of people celebrated on my birthday. They celebrated the birth of Christ. I was born on December 25th, 1951. It is such a blessing to be born on Christmas Day, and what is more special is that my youngest sister Noel is also born on Christmas Day, as is my nephew Fadi Ibrahim.

In my 60 plus years, my husband John and I have traveled to many places. Both within the United States and around the world. But in my life, there is no place like Zahle. In Zahle, you will find a melting pot of various Lebanese people of all religions, all different cultural statuses and more. But they all have one thing in common! Their love for delicious Lebanese cuisine, (our specialty is Taboule, Kibbee Naya, and Arak.)

Zahle is so special because the heavens shine on the valley 365 days of the year. The air is pure, fresh, and relaxing. The people are kind and gentle, friendly and welcoming. Truly there is no place like Zahle in the entire world.

As a child, my father Wadih at a young age was in the French military. He had the distinguished honor of serving as a general. My mother Georgette was originally from the north of Lebanon, from Akkar.

I have such treasured memories growing up in Zahle. As children we would often visit our neighbors in our township of Ma'alka. The Hatem family has for generations held elected positions in both Ma'alka and in Zahle. My family was large and very well respected. My father owned a lot of land throughout the Bekka Valley, land that is treasured to this day, and still remains in our family. The largest of grapes were grown on my father's land. Oh the memories of visiting all of my friends and family. I enjoyed as a child visiting my taunt Rashidi, my ammou Brahim, and one of my favorite aunts, taunt Georgette Makhoul. To this day, in fact just as recent as last fall I was so happy to visit with my aunt Georgette. Her smile reminded me of my special and blessed grandmother Haseebeh. My grandmother was a devoted Orthodox Christian. I was raised in a strict Maronite Catholic family, and the finest traditions where handed down to me as a child growing up in Zahle. Ah the days of living as a child in Lebanon, days that I shall cherish and never forget. I have been blessed to be a part of a truly special family. Allow me to take you on a stroll down memory lane. My oldest brother Victor, reminds me in so many ways of my late father Wadih. He is a kind and special man with such historic stories. His stories are filled with wisdom and love. I remember on a recent trip we gathered at the home of my brother Raymond and his lovely wife Amal and Victor sang us some traditional Lebanese folkloric songs at the dinner table. I sat and remembered my father singing when we were children so many years ago. My eldest sister, Lilly Hatem Haddad, is a remarkable lady. In life you will only meet one Lilly. She also reminds me of a life that doesn't exist anymore. Lilly has such a smile and such a passion about her. Many people have told us that we look a lot alike. My esteemed brother Edmone, who is older than I am, is by far one of the classiest most well respected business men that anyone will ever meet both in Lebanon and throughout the entire Arab world. Edmone, a distinguished gentleman that he is, always worked very hard, like all of my siblings to provide for the entire family. In the beginning of his diverse career Edmone and his lovely wife Renee began designing the most elegant and detailed dresses for almost all of the royal family of Saudi Arabia. Edmone later in life went into the business of our ancestors and grew the finest grapes in all of the Bekaa Valley to produce Arak and various wines. My brother Raymond and I grew up a world away from each other. For many years my older brother lived in Liberia, and worked in the restaurant and hotel industry, owning his own hotels. Sadly I did not have all too many memories of him as a child. Later in life I had the opportunity to really get to know he and his lovely wife Amal. I remember recently on my last visit to Beirut that Amal, my sister Josephine, my son Douglas and I toured the great museum of Saint George in the crypt below the Saint George Antiochian Orthodox Cathedral in downtown

Beirut. What a fun and exciting adventure that was. Much like the rest of my siblings Raymond always worked very hard to provide for his family and the entire family. He is a special and dear brother, and I cherish my memories of he and his family. Najla. Ya habibti Najla! Of all of my siblings, I particularly enjoy visiting with Najla. While she is very classy and elegant, she is also one of the most fun ladies I have ever met! Never will I forget the time that she, Renee and I visited a certain 'hot spot' in Jounieh, and we laughed the entire night away! Najla married one of the most popular and respected journalists in the entire country. My brother in law George Bachir. When you use the word 'fun' it very much describe's my sister Josephine. It was my pleasure and honor to have Josephine stand as my maid of honor at my wedding. Josephine is special to me like none other. One of the kindest ladies I have ever gotten to really be friends with is

Josephine. Josephine is humble, sweet and an amazing chef! I have a special place for all of my nieces and nephews but Adriana, Ibrahim and Fadi, yah Fadi, it has been my joy to have had such a blessed friendship with her children. All of my nephews and nieces are amazing. As a young child, my older sister Laure married at a young age. She traveled as a new bride to Brazil and built a large empire in the clothing industry. God Bless she and her husband Michel, today they own one of the largest clothing manufactures in all of South America, employing thousands of individuals. However much like my other siblings, Laure always has been kind, generous, and has never forgotten where she came from. She has always had one of the most beautiful voices I have ever heard. I remember as a child music producers from Beirut came to our home and wanted my parents to allow Laure to become an international singer. It was not meant to be but she always would sing the songs we learned in church. My older brother Freddy 'Fredo' left Lebanon at a very young age and traveled to Columbia to make a new life for himself. Fredo settled in Cartagena and became a major success in business and in the national government. Today we have cousins that have served nationally in the Columbian parliament. Sadly I have never actually met Fredo. I remember once many years ago I spoke briefly to him over the telephone and we both began to cry. Ironically I asked him, 'shou, laish em yipkee' (why are you crying?) and his response was 'shteht naylahk ouh aktar' (I miss you and then some) For a sibling that I never actually met, he has always had a place in my heart as if we have always known each other. One day, God willing I pray that the opportunity will come along that I may travel to Columbia to meet my brother. Tony, my younger brother by only a few years, is in a class by himself. Habibi Tony. I remember my nephew Pierre Bachir, Najla's son, once telling my younger son Douglas that Tony has an amazing heart. Tony is a strong, good person, a very intelligent man who has compassion like none other. While he is a strong man, he has been blessed to have an equally strong and amazing wife, Zoha. Habibti yah elbi Zoha. Zoha is my sister in law, but I have always loved her like a sister. She is a true ladies lady. Zoha has kept one of the finest households that anyone could ever keep. The most delicious and humble of meals are always prepared while Zoha often attends church daily. She truly is a remarkable and Christ filled friend to all whom she meets.

My brother Sammy was always and has always had a special place in my heart as well. He is a tall, strong intimidating man. I fondly remember growing up as Sammy's older sister. At a young age I used to run around our house and pinch Sammy & Tony's ears. They would hide throughout our family home, behind the couches, and such and I would always see them but pretend that I didn't. Those days of innocent adolescent fun are cherished like none other. Today Sammy has gone and also started a new chapter in his life building a successful business in Brazil. He is married and has two beautiful children, one of which he named in honor of our late mother. In every family you have that one sister or brother who is 'stunning' who could be in a room with hundreds, perhaps thousands of people and they would shine all on their own......For me, that is my sister Ousama. Ousama is perhaps one of the most beautiful ladies in all of Zahle, perhaps in all of Lebanon. Even as a new 'Tayta' (grandmother) she still is absolutely beautiful. She married a fine man, Tony, who together raised four wonderful children. I love my visits with Ousama because much like Lilly, Ousama reminds me of a time long ago, a time when we were all LEBANESE. No one spoke of religious differences, everyone genuinely loved one another. All of my siblings have one thing in common. LOVE. What is life without Love? My baby sister, who is also born on December 25th, Noel, is so unique and special to me just like all of my siblings. She has been blessed in many ways, and has showed and displayed love to all of us growing up in our family home. Noel is special particularly to me because when momma became older, and wasn't well, Noel and Zoha never left her side. To me that in itself is a beautiful gift.

-America-

Marriage and the early days in New Jersey and Florida

It was as if it was just yesterday that I remember the fall of 1971 meeting this interesting and good looking (I thought he was a bit of a hippy but that's between us....so shhhh....) young man from Brooklyn, New York. He came to visit our family home with his grandmother Alia Hatem, who was a distant cousin of my father Wadih. The first time I met John I found him to be charming, and funny. He was intelligent and had a smile to him that caught my eye. He didn't speak Arabic too well, and I didn't speak English all too well either. In those days in Beirut you really only needed to know 'habibi' (my sweet, my love, my dear) and 'misahtee' (money). Come to think of it, ironically in 2012, you still only need to know those two words to get through a day in

Lebanon! We got to know each other, and before you knew it we were married. I vividly remember it rained on our wedding day. It was November 18th, 1971. We were married at the Saint Nicholas Antiochian Orthodox Cathedral in Zahle. The same Archbishop who married us is still today the head of the archdiocese of Zahle. My sister Josephine was the maid of honor at our wedding and my cousin Antoine was John's best man. Ah it was as if the entire city of Zahle attended our wedding. Sadly John's parents were not able to attend as they were living in New Jersey. 'Tayta Alia' as I came to know her instantly became my friend. She was strong, kind and gentle all at the same time. At first it was very difficult leaving my family for the very first time. I was about to embark on a whole new journey, a whole new life in America! We spent an enjoyable honeymoon in Beirut and boarded a Pan American Airlines flight headed for New York.

I had never visited New York. I had watched movies about America, listened to popular music by Elvis and Frank Sinatra, but the idea of this whole new world was both exciting and sad at the time. My God, what a day it was at the Beirut International Airport. John was anxious to return home with me by his side. His young (and I'll be humbled to say beautiful new bride.) Tayta Alia was also tired and wanted to return home to her daughters Alyce and Virginia. Ah how I remember momma crying. My father stood strong and my siblings and cousins all accompanied us to the airport. I knew God had a plan for me, and it was a blessed plan at that.

One of many stories I will always remember was the flight to the United States. I recall the entire trip I was in tears. Yes I had just married this cute guy, this American Lebanese from 'Bay Ridge'.

However, at the same time I had never lived apart for any length of time from my family. Johnny ate both of our meals on the flight. According to the story Johnny shared with us, his grandmother was not too keen about the idea of flying across the ocean to get to Lebanon, so she wasn't too excited about flying back to New York. Oh I remember that, and in those days, airplane food was really nice. It wasn't like it is today. Even as nice as it was back in 1971, Tayta Alia was not in the mood to be asked whether she desired 'chicken or beef.' Upon landing at John F. Kennedy airport, what had to have been one of the most entertaining events occurred by chance. We walked off the plane and started to enter the line for customs and immigration. Here I was tired and at the same time anxious and excited. I was in a whole new world, for the first time ever! Johnny was tired and himself anxious. Well it came to be our turn in line to go through customs' and immigration. I walked through the line first, (see back then upon marrying Johnny, I was instantly issued a green card while still in Beirut.) so, all of a sudden I heard in the background Tayta Alia cursing and screaming at the customs agent in Arabic. Apparently if memory serves correctly, older ladies back in the early 70's carried a special container of facial powder that looked a lot like the illegal drug cocaine. I remember being greeted by Mama Alyce and Baba Edgar at the airport, and all the while Johnny abruptly told his mom to calm down her mother before they arrested her! The customs lady was an African American agent who didn't understand how an older Lebanese lady carried so much facial powder. While Tayta Alia was cursing her in the most unique of Zahle curses, the agent was not liking her tone and attitude too much. Thank God Mama Alyce was able to calm her mother down while at the same time she managed to defuse the situation. The beginning days of living in New Jersey quickly became enjoyable. I was truly blessed to have an amazing mother and father in law. Only weeks after our arrival to America, Mama Alyce and Baba Edgar gave Johnny and I a wonderful and warm wedding reception. What a large group of family and friends attended. It was so special to meet Mama Alyce's sister taunt Virginia, and her husband Gabe. I met my husband's charming first cousin Kenneth, and his wonderful brother Bobby. Mama Alyce had many friendly cousins. Uncle Elie, (who was also a distant cousin of mine) and his daughters Judy and Cathy. Her cousins Evelyn Shamoun and her sister Anne Moore, and many others.   I was so pleased to meet many of my 'new' families oldest friends. Mama Alyce was a pioneer in the Lebanese community like none other and she had a tremendous amount of friends. Some spoke Arabic and others did not. After a time period had passed, my husband attended Saint Vladimir's Theological Seminary and he was ordained a priest in the Orthodox Christian religion by one of the most holy and blessed bishops, Archbishop Michael Shaheen originally of Syira. Ah the memories of Sayidna Michael. He was such a humble and soft spoken man. Haram (so sad in Arabic) I remember well that Mama Alyce had wanted to take the Archbishop to dinner the evening that Johnny was ordained a priest, and the bishop simply requested her to make a home cooked meal of Kibbee Naya. After a brief period of time serving a parish in upstate New York, Johnny and I were given an opportunity to lead a new and growing church in Florida. After much prayer and upon hearing what God wanted we embarked on a whole new journey to a small city in Central Florida that was famous for Disney World, Orange groves and a lot of empty land. In the beginning Orlando was more of a small church, at the time having no actual church home. The early days saw us renting other church halls, and even funeral homes to serve the Divine Liturgy. I remember Johnny's cousin Kenny lived for a short period of time next door to us on Sherwood Court in Altamonte Springs. Kenny helped in many ways and worked one on one with Johnny to help our small church flourish in the mid 1970's. Time passed and before we knew it, Johnny and I were expecting our first child. As a young 'Abouna' (priest) and 'Khouriye' (wife of the priest) we worked very hard to build a new church. The early days of Saint George's were challenging and at times very difficult. Johnny had many visions. He established an actual Orthodox Christian chapel in the middle of a mall. Nothing like that had ever occurred. A small group from our small church used to feed the poor weekly and worked with the 'daily bread' and meals on wheel's program. How funny it is that 35 years ago, this same program has come back to Saint George's, being conducted right out of the church hall all over again, and being lead by an amazing true Christian disciple of Christ, a lovely lady, a convert to our faith, by the name of Rachelle. Additionally Johnny, at the time had the only Orthodox Christian radio and television show, and established over eight missions all over Florida. When our family wasn't building a community, we were traveling all over the state ministering to new communities. We were blessed to have as our first child, this amazing blonde curly haired baby boy, whom we named John Edgar, in honor of my husband. He was born on Thursday morning, (April 18th) in 1974. He had decided to keep me up most of the night on the 17th making his debut at the early hour of 7:45 in the morning! The early days of being both a new mom and a new wife of a priest were challenging. In the Holy Bible, a particular favorite verse of mine, in the book of Philippians, (4:13) says ‘I can do all things through Christ who Strengthens me.’ That verse was definitely written for priests and their families! My first child, Johnny (or as I often would call him ‘Little Johnny’) truly has to be one of the most intelligent , wise and sharp men I have ever known. Even as a young child it was as if he was always one step ahead of his peers. Not just in scholastics, but in life in general. Johnny and I often will sit and watch the business news on the evening news and it amazes me how intelligent he is. Johnny has gone through many trials and tribulations, yet he not only has come out on top, he continues to have the same bright and charming smile that he had the day he was born. I thank God for that gift he possess, that being his creative sense of humor.

Life soon became 'of the norm' for my new family. Orlando was fun, very relaxed, not like it is today. Yah Allah, (My God) I remember when we first came to Orlando as far as you could see

where orange groves and land. Today good luck finding land that doesn't have a Starbucks or a Wal-Mart on it! Challenges, like I said came and went. Times were difficult and times were good. We built a ministry together. Yes Johnny was the priest and yes Jesus blessed him to have the wisdom to accomplish all that he did. But I would like to meet one successful priest that didn't have an equally strong and wisdom filled wife on his side. Many days and many nights I remember my husband overcoming challenges and obstacles, and I stood as strong as I could to help him, and as best as I knew how. Remember, too often children enjoy being a part of the 'blame' game, the 'you did this or didn't do that' conversation is very popular in many households. Alas, I don't recall being given that 'book' on how to be the perfect wife, or mother. That's because there is no book. There is no class at the local community college. Parenthood is one of the most difficult callings ever. We did the best we could, we asked for God's guidance and for the most part most moms and dads, including myself are proud of what we accomplished. Before long, Jesus Christ had blessed me to be pregnant again, it was to be a boy. The year 1976 was filled with events that shaped Saint George's. Our small church was renting at the time our present day church home on Rosalind Avenue. We faced obstacles that we might lose the church building to the library next door. Johnny faced great difficulties. The owners of the church facility wanted to sell the building. At the time I was pregnant with my second son Douglas, and my father in law was very sick.

On June 7th, 1976 (and at an even earlier hour then my first pregnancy) I gave birth to my second child, my baby son Douglas. I often would tell Douglas that he had these beautiful 'bedroom eyes'.

At first my husband had to specially request from his mother and father to name our second son Douglas, after Johnny's late brother. Haram, in the summer of 1962 my brother in law, at the age of 19 was killed in a horrible accident. I never knew him, but so many stories were told to me as to what an amazing young man he truly was. He served honorably in the United States Marines. Mama Alyce agreed to give her blessing to name our second son after her late son, but requested that we change his middle name from Alexander, to George, in honor of our new church. And so we did. The next year was by far one that I shall never forget.

God Bless my mother in law. I feel she spent most of 1976 and 1977 tending to her husband Baba Edgar. He became more and more sick and sadly was called home to be with our Lord in 1977. I had never experienced the customs of a funeral in America. See in Lebanon, God forbid, when someone dies they are buried the next morning. In America it was a totally different scenario. The funeral for Baba Edgar was held at Saint George's and he was buried in Brooklyn, New York. Baba Edgar was such a distinguished man. I recently found out via a conversation with my son Douglas, that Baba Edgar was approached by executives in Hollywood and in New York City to join the ranks of Danny Thomas, Groucho Marks and others in the world of television comedy. I will share, with respect to our Lebanese friend Mr. Thomas, Baba Edgar was no Danny Thomas. In my opinion, and in the opinion of many many people who sat in the packed audiences in New York City that he regularly performed in, Edgar Hamatie was truly one of the funniest most entertaining comedians and concert pianists. Not only did Edgar have a gift of accents and 'timing' he would sit at the piano and the concert hall would be literally lit up. 'Ed' or 'Eddie' as he was known, often times would 'rescue' businesses, i.e. night clubs and dinner venues. I remember hearing from many people that if a large venue in Manhattan wasn't doing too well with its patrons, that they would call upon 'Edgar Hamatie' to come and rescue them. This man would literally pack the house like no one else. His gift of playing the piano was unheard of. Edgar came from a long line of entertainers. If you have a brief minute, for those of you who have an 'iPhone' go to what's known as 'iTunes' and look up a man named 'Naim Karakand'. Jiddo Naim, Edgar's step-father and a man who was very influential in Edgar's life, was one of the most, if not the most famous Middle Eastern violinist in the history of the United States. Edgar's mother, Hananee Karakand truly lit up a concert hall in her esteemed gift of entertainment. Hananee performed in the largest venues during the turn of the century, she was herself a Hollywood legend and even entertained for the president of the United States at the time, Woodrow Wilson. Edgar, being a truly humbled man was quoted as telling those talent & casting agents that he did not want to neglect or take away time from his family.

That had he chosen a life that was offered to him, to act in television shows and movies, that he would have not been able to be the father that he had always dreamed of. My husband often speaks of his father, particularly of his talent, but more so, that he truly was a great 'man' and an even greater 'father'. Although my time with him as his daughter in law was brief, Johnny was definitely right, he was an amazing friend and a true Christian man.

It was a very difficult and sad period for my new family. As God takes in life, he also always blesses in life. Not long after my father in law's passing I was pregnant and this time it was to be a girl. I went into labor the last time (with Douglas) a little on the scared side of things. I recall our family friend Joyce Joseph at the time lived a few minutes from Johnny and I. When I went into labor with Douglas, when my water broke, I called Joyce to come and wake up Johnny. She tip toed into our bedroom and in her strong (Norwood) Boston way of speaking, she shouted 'FATHER JOHN' WAKE UP! And so we went off to the hospital. Alas, this time it was different. I went into labor, it was late September of 1978, I was at our church with Mama Alyce, Joyce and Kenny Joseph and Stella Sirks, and Johnny was at a clergy event in Pennsylvania. I felt that I was alone, but I knew that Jesus Christ was with me the entire time. Often in life we forget that we are never alone. One could understand the fears of going into labor and your husband isn't at your side. I had a safe and easy delivery and God had blessed us with a beautiful baby girl named Marie Antoinette. So many memories I have, in fact I remember Johnny wrote such a beautiful letter to me, filled with such blessed words. It was a personal letter, and I still have that letter to this day. I've kept it, special to my heart. He felt so sad that he had missed the birth of our third child and our first daughter. He came directly from the airport in the middle of the night, having written that personal letter while on the flight from Pennsylvania.

The years passed and life became 'normal' as I was pregnant with my fourth child, Anastasia, an absolutely beautiful baby, with the whitest skin, the most beautiful curly hair, our church family grew. We became so close with so many of the original founding families. Harvey and Evelyn Reich, Sam and Mary David, Ken and Joyce Joseph, Eugene and Judy Volik, and of course my favorite family from Greece, Tom and his lovely wife Janice Maillis. These people were our family. We also had many Lebanese & Syrian friends. Virginia Ballestero, (she went on to become such a sister to me) Tony and Norma Herro, (they lived in an area at the time known as 'little Syria') Georgette Hachem, Freddy, Bella and Jeanette Hage, Astori & Margaret Shaleesh, George Klele, and his fun daughters Patty and Gabby, Nasri and

Najat Sawaya (Nasri and Najat were like one of our best friends when we first came to Orlando, it was at their home that I called

Mama Alyce and Baba Edgar to tell them I was pregnant with Johnny). To list all of the people we truly called our 'Orlando' family would take pages and pages. Mama Alyce had her own 'new' friends, who also quickly became our friends. Her best friend, Florence was also one of our best friends. The Syrian Lebanese Club of Orlando was established at 'Mum Becky's' (Aunt Becky) house originally mum Becky lived in a beautiful older home and then she and Florence moved to an equal lovely home on Hazelwood drive in the downtown area of Orlando. Florence was definitely one of the most generous and kind ladies I had ever met in my entire life. So many Friday's we would go to mum Becky's home and eat. No one ever called, we just went and ate, and ate and ate and ate! We would run into friends at mum Becky's house. Bella and Jeanette Hage were regulars, our dear friend Helen Jones and her daughter Liz, we would see everyone

at the club away from the club. All were welcomed. Seeing as the club was originally established at mum Becky's house, it eventually built a large official clubhouse on Mills avenue, but in the end of the day it was at her home that everyone always felt a warm welcome. I truly enjoyed the 'good ole days'. Jesus blessed Johnny and I to have our fifth and final child. A beautiful baby girl named Alexandra. Five was enough! By the mid to late 1980's Saint George's was a flourishing congregation. We had many events that were most enjoyable. The fiesta in the park, the International Dinner that was held every year. Weekend dinners at Tony & Virginia Ballesteros' home in Kissimmee. We used to enjoy taking our children to the famous 'A-Train' restaurant, that was owned by Virginia and Tony. Oh how many meals were we invited to and never saw a bill. Virginia and Tony truly made our family feel blessed and welcomed. What a fun and entertaining

family the Ballestero's where and still are. Her son Angelo went on to become a singing success and has a ministry in one of Orlando's largest church's and her daughter Virginia Anne, who I always liked to call 'Sunshine' went on to become a great business success story. What fun we would have after great dinners when we would all gather upstairs in Angelo's amazing studio and he would sing his latest hits for us. I had a special relationship with Tony's mom, taunt Antoinette. We still have the beautiful custom dolls that she brought for my three daughters from Brazil. She was truly a 'ladies lady'. A classy and soft spoken lady. I sit back and remember the good times with our friend Harvey. Harvey was for some time married to Evelyn, yet he was 'unique' to our circle of friends because he was not of the Lebanese Orthodox Christian 'group'. He was born and raised in the Jewish religion. However, in all of my years meeting people and becoming friends

with people, I never met anyone as special, kind and funny as Harvey Reich. It was a true loss for our community when Harvey was called home recently to Christ's heavenly kingdom. Later in life, Harvey actually converted to the Orthodox Christian religion and he had specially requested Mama Alyce to be his God mother. The time passed and Johnny had decided to take our entire family to visit Lebanon. I remember people in our church being concerned for us to travel to Lebanon in the summer of 1984. There was a war going on and it was a bad war at that. Jesus

Christ opened the doors for us and we embarked on an amazing journey in August of 1984. It was the first time that my entire family in Zahle would meet all five of my children. I was very

excited. I was also a little nervous. All in all we had a blessed journey filled with many wonderful memories. My son's

remember meeting my special grandmother Haseebee. It was a brief and memorable encounter. To this day, I still carry with me the beautiful and last picture I ever took with her. In it we are standing in front of the entrance gate to her home. I was wearing a light purple dress that day, with a small red rose in the corner. She was wearing a long sleeved black dress. At first glance of her beautiful smile I began to cry. I was so happy to embrace my own Tayta. In her soft spoken voice she simply said 'yah ah abournee' 'yah hayateeh' while these words are semi difficult to translate, any special granddaughter of our culture knows these words all too well, spoken by many of our parents and grandparents. It would be the last time I saw my grandmother, the last time I embraced her, the last time I felt the softness of her kiss. But in my heart all of these years later, she has always been my true

guardian angel. For throughout the rest of the 1980's wonderful and challenging things occurred for myself and my family. For the first time in years it was apparent to our family that we had outgrown our humble and cozy home in Altamonte Springs. Jesus blessed my husband once again with a vision in finding a much larger and spacious home only minutes away in what is known as the city of Maitland. We moved into this large home and began a new life in a new area. It was difficult at first, as we had become very comfortable with the surroundings of Altamonte Springs.

Many young moms have mother in laws that could be construed as challenging. I however was blessed with a mother in law that was a true gift from God. Having lived next door to her for many many years also was a blessing like none other. Mama Alyce was so special to me. I cannot remember how many days our entire family would go next door to be welcomed with her warm

hospitality. She would prepare meals made from the finest Lebanese ingredients. Not only did she always welcome my children with anything they needed. She always made me feel special. In fact often times she would publicly tell people I was the daughter she never had. As if dinners was not enough,

she would take me grocery shopping all the time, often times she would pay for groceries and not allow me to pay. She always made sure to help by taking my children to the dentist, to events in the community and all the while she always respected me as not just being the children's mom, but also as the 'Khouriye' of Saint George's. Mama Alyce sang in the choir, served on the parish council, was for decades the superintendent of the church school at Saint George's and of course was the ladies guild president. Yet, at the end of the day she was the kindest most

generous mother, mother in law and grandmother that any family could ever wish for. As the late 1980's progressed, the year 1989 was a very busy year for me, and sadly not in a good way. In the beginning of the year uncle Gabe, taunt Virginia Khouri's husband died unexpectedly. This was particularly sad for me because it had been a long time since a member of my 'new' family had died. Mama Alyce, Johnny and I drove the day uncle Gabe died to be with taunt Virginia in Boca Raton. I remember that day well. Sadly, only a few months later, my first ever friend in America, Tayta Alia also died. God Bless Mama Alyce. She was such a good daughter to her mother. She would take her mother home cooked Lebanese meals three times a week to the assisted living facility that she resided in for years. Mama Alyce in the beginning, in fact for many years took care of her mother and always made her feel more then welcomed in her home. Towards the later years in life Taytya Alia became semi crippled and Mama Alyce could not physically assist her mother with her daily needs. It was beyond difficult on her that her mother spent her later years in life what was known as the 'Florida Manor' but, indeed it was one of the finest senior homes in the community and she truly did so much for her mother, when her mother died it was a dark day for her. This was also difficult for my children because it was the first time they themselves had lost a member of our immediate family. While the 1980's kept us so busy, we consecrated our church home and we had the blessing of having Sayidna 'Bishop in Arabic' Michael Shaheen to officiate at this most blessed event, my husband and I also had a few fun trips. We traveled to the inauguration of President George H.W. Bush with Kenny and his lovely wife Mary Ellen Khouri, and we enjoyed fun trips to the Bahamas to visit old friends. The 1990's came and God blessed our family and our church with many good things. It was a time period of good memories. Johnny and I last traveled to Lebanon in 1989 with our two sons. During the period of the 1990's we had not visited Lebanon for almost nine years. One of the darkest days for me was the day my father died. He had been blessed to live to the age of 96. I was very saddened by his passing and more so that I couldn't be with my family in Zahle. Time had passed and Johnny and I decided to visit Lebanon once again. It was my first trip home that I would not see my father Wadih. It was also our first trip back to my country since the end of the civil war. What a mess Beirut was. What a haram Lebanon had become. Lebanese had killed each other. How could the most beautiful country in the world become so torn apart? I never did understand the western media regarding 'Muslims and Christians'

in the Middle East. When we were children our best friends were Muslims and Christians. I grew up with our neighbors in Zahle who were Muslim. They had a daughter named Zeina. As far back as the age of 8 years old, Zeina and I would eat from the same plate. We would enjoy Okra and rice. Funny thing, even today in America, two of my oldest and dearest friends, Hassan and Samya Hafza, are just the same as Zeina and I where. My son and I always go to Hassan's and we eat, laugh, joke compare stories, stroll down memory lane. NOT as people of different faith's or differences, but as LEBANESE. We never asked as children, 'are you a Sunni Muslim, a Shi'ite Muslim, are you Christian Orthodox or Christian Maronite.? We were Lebanese and we lived as one. Yet not everyone in Lebanon thought like that. Beirut was an absolute mess. I remember my brother Tony Hatem, and brother in law Tony Bsaibess picking Johnny and I

up at the airport and driving us to Zahle, and I recall that I couldn't stop counting the destroyed buildings in Beirut. You have to understand that on our last trip in 1989, we traveled into Damascus and not into Beirut. After all, the war was very bad in areas of Beirut. Life in Zahle had not changed. The people were as warm and welcoming as ever. Years came and years went. My children grew up, they were college aged and life was once again progressing.

Before I knew it, time had passed, and on my son's birthday I received a call, one that no daughter wants to receive. My mother Georgette had died. I remember that I tried the best I could not to tell my son on his birthday. But, he knew something was wrong and embraced me. It was a hug that I shall never forget. We went on that night to celebrate his birthday, and I remember when

Johnny had come home that day, and Douglas had gone outside to greet him. He simply said 'Tayta Georgette died' and I remember Johnny was very sad for me that warm summer day. Many wonderful memories occurred during the next few years. Our children enjoyed summers at the church camp known as the Antiochian Village in Pennsylvania. One summer in particular my husband had purchased a car for myself, my two sons, and my eldest daughter to drive up north in. Not 75 miles out of Orlando, the car had mechanical issues and we called Johnny and he went and rented a late model car and drove it to the gas station that we were stuck at. I remember thinking to myself, and then saying out loud, 'how will you get back to Orlando?' and Johnny calmly said, 'I'll figure it out, I just want you all to get to Pennsylvania on time.' That was a memory, a short story that I will always remember.

We had become comfortably settled in our life in Maitland. In the late 1990's our family was blessed with the marriage of my eldest daughter Marie Antoinette, who married one of the most amazing young men any mom could ever wish to call a son in law.

Sharif and his family were for many years a part of our church family. So when my daughter and he began dating it was a warm and pleasant blessing for us all. In time they were engaged and married and almost all of the community came to their beautiful wedding.

People traveled from far away to attend the event. The reception was held at the Syrian Lebanese American Club. Interestingly enough it was the last event ever held at the famous 'SLAC' on Mills avenue. My daughter never looked so beautiful as she had on that day. Taunt Virginia and her son Kenneth traveled to be at the wedding, so did our cousins from Fort Lauderdale, the Bitar family. Many of our old and new friends attended and it was truly a blessed event. It was a great joy to witness the marriage of my eldest daughter. She lived up to her namesake 'Queen Marie Antoinette'.

Time passed, and after a few years, we lost our beloved taunt Virginia Khouri, it was a cold and sad day in January when she was called home to be with the Lord. But nothing prepared us for the loss of both of my children's God parents within months of each other in the year 2006. Virginia Ballestero had been having challenging times with her ailments. She had only recently lost her beloved husband Tony, who was such a remarkable business man. Virgie, as I called her, taught me many things. She would always tell me to be strong. To be CHRIST like. Her words were filled with the Holy Spirit. At her funeral, I cried tears filled with many many years of memories. I couldn't believe that such an angel had gone all too soon. What a remarkable lady Virginia Ballestero truly was. But, like all things in life, nothing at all prepared me for the loss of Kenny. No one saw that coming. In the month of March, he had been with us to grieve at the passing of Virgie. He looked and appeared to be in great health. At the conclusion of her funeral, we had all walked outside of the church and let a lot of balloons into the open air. Virgie loved balloons and 'Betty Boop' the famous cartoon character, so my youngest son Douglas, went and purchased a dozen Betty Boop balloons. I learned initially of his illness in May of 2006, and by June I had spoken briefly to he and his beloved wife Mary Ellen. It all happened too fast. I didn't have the proper chance to tell him what an impact he was on my life.

He was like a brother to me. A special friend, a true disciple of Christ. July was a dark and lonely month. Kenny had died and I never got to thank him for thirty plus years of being such a good person and friend. I remember my strong and blessed son in law drove us all through the night to be at Kenny's funeral in Mount Pocono. There wasn't a dry eye at the funeral. The world had lost one of the finest Christians ever. After the funeral of Kenny, our family drove to nearby Brooklyn and we visited some of the sights in New York. It was a difficult drive down memory lane.

Years had passed, life was progressing, my children were growing up before my eyes and God had truly given me amazing blessings. My beloved daughter Marie Antoinette and her husband Sharif had our first grandchild, a boy named Isaac. Much is to be said about Izookey! As I like to call him. He is the light of my eye. Never a day goes by that Isaac doesn't make smile. It is such a joy to be a part of his life. He is truly a blessing from Jesus Christ.

God does not give us more then we can handle. Let me tell you that first hand. However, the most difficult days lay ahead for me, not only as a wife, but mainly as a mother. I will briefly, or rather humbly share that Jesus Christ never left my side during the tragic days, weeks and months that my eldest son Johnny was in the hospital. For years I had watched on television, and had sympathized with mothers and fathers whose children had become sick or endured tragedies. I always felt internally that those tragedies would or could not happen to my family. What my son Johnny went through was literally hell on earth. Jesus Christ was with us the entire time. From the moment we arrived at the small hospital in New Smyrna beach to the long and difficult days in Gainesville. Days, weeks and months of fear, of not knowing what lay ahead next. Watching my son suffer truly crushed me inside. It was and to this day is one of the most difficult time periods I ever endured. Not a day goes by that I don't thank Jesus for giving my son the strength and will power to progress in his life. He is so strong, and is himself a role model for my entire family. I know for sure that no one in the Hamatie or Hatem family could possibly have endured what he went through. May God bless him always for that strength. I cannot even begin to thank the people who came so far to be with our family. The Joseph's, my sister in Christ, Samya Sadek, and our true sister Georgette Hachem. The list is so long, not a Sunday didn't go by that many in our church family, Nick and Fran, Mary Moore, and many others didn't constantly remind us that Johnny was in their daily prayers. Like I always say, all of my children are amazing, but my eldest is truly blessed with the gift of strength and wisdom.

One of my most cherished journeys was when my youngest daughter Alexandra invited me to the most magical land on earth. As a proud Lebanese, I will always think of Lebanon as the most beautiful place, but one has to visit the magical land known as Hawaii…. Alexandra had invited me to visit the islands of Hawaii, particularly Maui, and we toured the state as if we were royalty. Everywhere we visited we made new and lifelong friends. We met missionaries' we met the 'locals' and we had such a remarkable time. The missionaries' insisted that we stay with them during our visit. I will always cherish that special time with my baby daughter.

Before I realized it, life had begun to return to normal.

Marie Antoinette had become pregnant again. And again it was to be a son. Our family was excited. Johnny and I would become grandparents yet again. Douglas was busy working on a series of fiction novels, and my daughters Anastasia and Alexandra were busy as ever. It was beginning to be a year like any other year. 2009 would be the year that I would be a Tayta yet again and I was becoming very excited. On Isaac's birthday, in March of 2009 the entire family attended his birthday party, including our cousins Bobby Khouri and his lovely wife Christine, (one of my best and most beloved friends). Little did we know that only a few weeks later, our family would truly suffer one of the greatest losses ever. We had no idea that the photograph we took at

Isaac's birthday party would be one of the last we would take as an entire family.

That Palm Sunday, it was the 12th of April - 2009, was like any other Palm Sunday. Our family was together at church, we had celebrated the Divine Liturgy together, and we walked around our church three times, as is customary in the Orthodox Christian tradition. Two days later, on the 14th of April, Jesus Christ called my mother in law home to his heavenly kingdom. What a day it was. Sharif, Marie Antoinette (who was pregnant at the time) Anastasia, her then boyfriend Clint, my son Johnny and I spent the early part of that tragic day at our family home in Maitland. Douglas was living at the time in New York City and Alexandra was living in Los Angeles. It was as if time had stood still. No one could realize what had happened. Mama Alyce was not sick, nor did she have any major ailments. She simply went to sleep Monday evening, and passed away during the night. I can only imagine the thoughts that went through my husband's mind upon going to wake up his beloved mother and she had gone home to be with our Lord unexpectedly. See I had known Mama Alyce on an intimate level as her daughter in law for a longer period of time then I had known my own mother. I came to America as a young bride, at the age of nineteen. Almost every day of all those years, I spent with Mama Alyce. Sure we had traveled to Greece, Lebanon, Syria, the Holy Land, the Caribbean and beyond, but when I didn't see her, we at least spoke. Johnny would always call to check on his mother. I guess subconsciously we always thought she would be with us forever. I didn't understand a world without Mama Alyce in it physically.

For a few years I had personally lived with her, in her home in Altamonte Springs taking care of her, before she moved into our family home in Maitland.

This was the lady who taught me many things in life. This was the lady who always made me feel like I was her daughter. I remember many times she would stand strong for me, as not just her daughter in law, but as her friend. She was a mentor, a teacher, but mainly someone that I had grown so close to. I couldn't imagine life without Mama Alyce. The days that followed happened to be Holy Week. Somehow with the blessings of God almighty, my husband managed to properly conduct all of the services during Holy Week and Pascha. The week that followed, that Saturday, our church was filled to capacity. We held the funeral of our beloved Mama Alyce. Old friends, new friends, family from far away all came to bid one last farewell to the true 'matriarch' of our family. It was Mama Alyce's generosity that helped us to acquire the large church home we have today. It was her generosity in so many ways that helped my husband and I when we first started out.

God Bless that little lady

from Bay Ridge Brooklyn. She quietly took care of all of the medical bills for the hospitalization when all of my five children were born. One cannot remember all she did, and losing her, much like Kenny, not being able to properly say goodbye was in itself one of the most difficult challenges for me. Each of my children spoke at her funeral. Hundreds came to bid her a final goodbye. We traveled to Brooklyn for the burial at Greenwood cemetery. She was laid to rest next to Baba Edgar, and her son Douglas Alexander. A part of my heart will always be with the most special lady that she truly was. To this day I see pictures of her and begin to think about what was some of the best years of my life. Mama Alyce, as my husband often would say, was truly an 'institution'. She was a remarkable lady. Ah the journey down memory lane. To be a part of the Hamatie family is to have such wonderful memories. Baba Edgar was a comedian! He always had funny stories and jokes to tell. Uncle Gabe, always wore a light blue blazer jacket, had a cigar in his mouth, and used to call my eldest daughter 'Tony'. He was such a good looking and charming man. He loved to play gin rummy at the famous '21' club. He and taunt Virginia would always stop over Mama Alyce's house for a brief night on their long drive down from New Jersey to Boca Raton. The good ole days were truly the best of days. The hafli's (Arabic Parties) were always fun in Orlando. The church picnic's in Downey Park with my children playing with aunt Helen Jones' grandchildren were always filled with fun memories. The many events at the Syrian Lebanese club. Oh the days of the SLAC on Mills avenue. I remember well the infamous Thursday poker nights. With Mama Alyce and Florence playing poker with Mr. Jammal, Adele Azar, Sara Deeb, Freddy Hage, and many others. The days when Kenny used to live in Altamonte Springs and we would meet with mum Becky and go to Sunday dinners at the Purple Porpoise, (which was owned by a friendly Lebanese man who we only knew as Mr. Bashir) Lord Chumlies, or the famous Ponderosa restaurant in Altamonte. The days of piling the children into Mama Alyce's Oldsmobile and going to 'Arthur Treachers' and enjoying a delicious fish dinner, only comparable to the days today taking my grandson's to Najat's famous Maryland fried chicken restaurant. Who could forget the multiple times we would go and sit and drink Arabic coffee for hours at Tony's Deli on 17-92. Norma Herro was and always will be one of the finest Lebanese chefs in history. Memories will and always shall be kept alive as long as we speak of them. How many years did Jesus bless me to help at our church? When I was a young mother, I would accompany my husband at least twice a week to go to the church and God gave me the strength and will power to clean our church. Before we had cleaning crews, as we call them today, there was 'Monique's crew', which consisted of just myself physically, and Jesus Christ spiritually. I used to sweep, and mop the downstairs hall, and vacuum the upstairs sanctuary. How I remember literally seeing Saint Herman in our church, as well as the Virgin Mary. Don't think for a minute that I 'thought' I saw them, or I imagined that I saw them. Believe me, they appeared to me and I embraced them, just as I did my late Tayta. All the while I simply did the best I could to tend to the needs of my five children and have a home cooked meal for our family every day. Never shall I forget, as I said earlier, about the many many meals Mama Alyce blessed us with. I don't know how I would have managed without her help. With all of the memories of the 'good ole days' some good, some sad, God has blessed us with a whole new generation of

'new and fun' memories.

My children these past few years have grown with me. I have been blessed with strength and wisdom that I never thought I had. I truly love children and always have enjoyed being around them. Many years ago Saint George's had a daily nursery academy for a short period of time. I was a part of that nursery, working daily to help it grow. Later in life I took a full time job working at a child care facility near to Mama Alyce's home. For a brief period of time I was blessed to be a live in nanny for one of my oldest friends. In the early 1970's Johnny and I became friends with Najat and Nasri Sawaya. Who would know that years later I would briefly become the live in nanny for their granddaughter Nicolette? See life gives us many chances and also gives us many tests to see what we can accomplish, what we can go through and how we can grow. New and exciting memories have already occurred. In the same year that we lost Mama Alyce, we were blessed to welcome my second and beloved grandson Jacob. I cannot explain how often I see his smile and I see Mama Alyce's smile, one in the same. He is such a special good looking young man. Ah the new memories we create every day. While Jesus called home my sister in Christ Virginia Ballestero, he blessed us with another amazing lady, a sister like none other. My dear friend Louella Cardoos. Louella, much like Virginia and Mama

Alyce is one of the kindest most enjoyable people I've ever met. Sadly she is only in Florida for about five months a year, but none the less when she is in Orlando she always welcomes my entire family for lazy days at the clubhouse pool, and delicious home cooked Arabic meals at her lovely house. Ah the best has yet to come. Recently, during a phone conversation with one of my oldest friends in Brooklyn, LuLu Sayeg, LuLu asked me the following........ 'shou Monique, anjahd you wrote a book?' I answered with a silent smile. While I have had the pleasure to write this brief story filled with memories of my life, some beautiful poetry that I wrote and others that have meant a lot to me, and of course my favorite home cooked Lebanese recipies,

the stories you all have read today were possible because of my love for Jesus Christ. In life we endure many obstacles. Believe me, that is a true statement. But, if you have a real faith in God, you can get through them all. One does not have to be wealthy in dollar bills, in homes, in the physical things. Sure that helps in many ways, but it will not get you salvation in Christ's heavenly kingdom. I personally am a multi-millionaire. But, not in dollars. I am a millionaire in friends, in memories, in blessings, in LIFE! And I thank Jesus Christ for that every single day of the year.

2012........ what a year it's going to be....

Kisses and hugs........ **Monique**, the **Zahle** Princess!

Some of my favorite poetry, some that I have written, and some that has had a major impact on my life, that I have borrowed...

My most beloved Lebanon, my journey home to Beirut by the Taboule Princess.... (Monique W. Hamatie)

It took me 10 years to see my beautiful family. I went back after 10 years to the heart of Zahle, my home sweet home. Zahle from the heart... I 'have' the best time of my life with my family.

Yum Yum! To the Arak! Zahle, you are so unique.

I don't know how people don't go back home?

Beirut ya Beirut, you are the luxury of family, the luxury of culture, the luxury of LOVE. The luxury of style, and much much more... I hope I will go back again.

BLESSINGS are God's gifts to us. Simple or great they are Produced by the over flow of his great love, we recognize these most often when include a reprieve from sickness or a financial provision for a critical need..... But, we are proven to take for granted the sunshine that lights our days and our spirits the affection of friends and family... the kindness of strangers...

Every good and perfect gift is from above coming down from the father of the heavenly lights. Who does not change like shifting shadows. Every blessings all around you are to encourage you to bask in the loving kindness of our awesome God. It is our prayer that as you move through these pages you will see God's hand in every aspect of your life filling it with goodness.

'Faith, Hope, Prayer, Charity, Peace, Belief'

'Love, Joy, Grace, Care, Life, Wisdom and to all Enter HIS Kingdom....

Thank you so much, and all my heartfelt love....

Monique W. Hamatie

My favorite Lebanese recipe....

Tabouli.....

(which interestingly enough originated in Zahle)

This is the real Lebanese Tabouli which you will notice has little Bulgur in it. There are two kinds of Bulgur: fine or coarse, and for Tabouli we use fine. You can find fine Bulgur in Lebanese/Middle Eastern grocery stores. Lebanese like to eat their Tabouli with crisp hearts of romaine lettuce. Our family in Zahle also enjoys cabbage as a way to eat Tabouli. It's so refreshing, especially on a hot summer day! Try mixing the salt and pepper with the chopped onions before adding them to the other ingredients; it brings out the sweet juice of the onion.

You will need the following:

3 bunches finely chopped flat leaf parsley

1 cup chopped fresh mint

2-3 tablespoons fine bulgur

1 chopped firm tomato

1/2 onion or 2 scallions chopped

1/2 cup extra Virgin olive oil

1/4 cup fresh lemon juice

salt and pepper to taste

1/2 teaspoon cayyene pepper (optional)

So, now you have your special ingredients, well what do you do next?

(shwaye shwaye habibi, as my sister Lilly would say....)

If you are going to prepare it in the special Zahle way, you should be at the home of Najat & Nasri Sawaya, while Najat, Norma Herro and myself gather in the kitchen, Johnny, Tony Herro and Nasri Sawaya can sit and discuss religion and politics out by the pool (a little humor always makes for a fun preparation!)

Prepare the chopped parsley and mint and set aside.

In a large bowl, mix Bulgur, chopped tomatoes, chopped onions/scallions with lemon juice, salt and pepper. Add to them the parsley and mint and olive oil and mix, adjusting seasoning by adding more oil and lemon if desired.

Serve cold garnished with romaine lettuce. If memory serves correctly, Norma would hopefully have made her delicious Kibbe Sineye (baked Kibbe) and Najat would have prepared her famous Hummos and Kibbe Nayae. The tabouli is always best with a cold glass of Arak. Not to be outdone of course by the enjoyment of some delicious Baht lahwah (Baklava)

My friends, it has been my absolute humble pleasure in sharing a brief 'story' of the first sixty years of my life. I have been so blessed and words cannot describe those blessings. Just last year my second daughter Anastasia married her fiancé Clinton. It was such a pleasure, such an honor to see our family grow. Anastasia truly looked like a princess. Life has been challenging, but I stand strong and I will, with Jesus by my side take one day at a time always. My youngest son Douglas always reminds me what a pure and genuine heart I truly have. And I always simply reply 'thank God' 'thank God.' I know God has a plan for my future, as he does your future. I am also well aware that life is difficult, life is scary at times, but it also is filled with great opportunities and chances. I have been so blessed to have many God children. Suzanne Tyndall, Heather and Michael Cameron, and many others. Don't ever live in fear, and always remember two things. Jesus Christ will always be there for you, and if you are reading my story, always know that you'll always have me as your

special friend.

Love Always,

Monique

www.ingramcontent.com/pod-product-compliance
Ingram Content Group UK Ltd.
Pitfield, Milton Keynes, MK11 3LW, UK
UKHW051136260726
13967UKWH00010B/3087

9 781105 722608